HEADstart

BATTLES

First published in Great Britain by
CAXTON EDITIONS
an imprint of
The Caxton Book Company,
16 Connaught Street,
Marble Arch, London, W2 2AF.

ISBN 1 84067 028 2

A copy of the CIP data for this book is available from the British Library upon request.

With grateful thanks to Helen Courtney

Created and produced for Caxton Editions by
FLAME TREE PUBLISHING,
a part of The Foundry Creative Media Company Ltd,
Crabtree Hall, Crabtree Lane,
Fulham, London, SW6 6TY.

Printed in Singapore by Star Standard Industries Pte. Ltd.

HEADstart

BATTLES

*The World's Major
Battles Explained in
Glorious Colour*

KAREN SULLIVAN

CAXTON EDITIONS

Contents

Introduction

A battle is a clash between groups of armed people. Battles can take place within countries (these are called 'intranational' battles or wars) or between countries (then called 'international'). Wars are generally caused by political problems or over difficulties with the economy. Political problems are those concerned with the governing of a country or state; economic problems are those concerned with money and other areas of finance. Wars are also fought over highly emotional issues such as religion and moral beliefs.

Before the use of gunpowder, land battles were mostly fought by hand-to-hand combat, using bows and arrows, swords, knives, spears, javelins and maces (a kind of club). For this reason, battles were generally quite short, because both men and horses tired very quickly. Also, the number of casualties was normally fairly low in proportion to the number of men who were fighting.

Gunpowder altered the nature of battles permanently in several ways. Bullets can travel over a long distance, and gunpowder made it possible to kill an enemy hundreds of metres away. Gunpowder also greatly increased the number of casualties in war and made the deaths of civilians (those people who were not involved in the fighting) far more likely.

Several centuries later, a new invention outclassed even gunpowder: the bomb. Bombs could be set off from a great distance and, with the invention of aeroplanes, they could be dropped from the air, killing hundreds of people and destroying vital property and land. Nuclear weapons brought even more serious consequences. They can travel over even greater distances and, by flicking a switch or giving a command, one individual has the power to kill thousands of people and devastate whole countries.

Great Wars Through History

Important Wars

c. 1200 BC Trojan Wars

499-479 BC Persian Wars

431-404 BC Peloponnesian War

334-323 BC Wars of Alexander the Great

264-241, 218-202, 149-146 BC Punic Wars

1096-1291 Crusades

1337-1453 Hundred Years' War

1455-1485 Wars of the Roses

1568-1648 Dutch Independence

1618-1648 Thirty Years' War

1642-1649 Civil War in England

1700-1721 Northern War

1701-1713 Spanish Succession

1740-1748 Austrian Succession

1756-1763 Seven Years' War

1775-1783 American Revolution

1789-1815 French Revolution & Napoleonic Wars

1812-1814 War of 1812

1821-1829 Greek Independence

1846-1848 Mexican War

1850-1865 Taiping Rebellion

1854-1856 Crimean War

The great battles throughout history have almost always been part of longer-term wars. More than 5,000 years ago, in the wars between civilizations of the Middle East, foot soldiers were the main combatants. This is still true today, except that modern infantrymen are supported by aircraft, artillery, tanks, and sophisticated communications systems. The timeline below lists some of the important wars across history, in which many key battles were fought.

1861–1865 Civil War in the United States
1866 Austro-Prussian War, or Seven Weeks' War
1870–1871 Franco-Prussian War
1877–1878 Russo-Turkish War
1894–1895 Chinese-Japanese War
1898 Spanish-American War
1899–1902 Boer War
1904–1905 Russo-Japanese War
1912–1913 Balkan Wars
1914–1918 First World War
1917–1918 Russian Revolution
1936–1939 Spanish Civil War
1939–1945 Second World War
1948–1949 First Arab-Israeli War
1950–1953 Korean War
1955–1975 Vietnam War
1956 Second Arab-Israeli War
1967 Six-Day War
1973 Yom Kippur War
1979–1989 Afghan Civil War
1980–1988 Iran-Iraq War
1991 Persian Gulf War

Early Battles: the Birth of Civilization to AD 500

In the great battles of early history, defeated warriors often fled, or escaped; they knew that if they were captured they would be put to death or sold as slaves. The Assyrians, who lived in what is now Iraq in about 1300 to 600 BC, were fierce and disciplined fighters, and as a result were very successful in battle. The ancient Egyptians, Greeks and Romans also had highly developed and skilled armies.

In early battles, foot soldiers, or 'infantry', were extremely important, but in about 2000 BC, the use of horses became more frequent. Early horses were not strong enough to be ridden by armoured warriors, so instead they were used to pull chariots. Charioteering, however, was expensive, so only the wealthy could use them. Later, horses became stronger and in about 900 BC soldiers began to ride horses into battle. These mounted warriors were known as the 'cavalry'.

Most of the key battles of early history were fought for much the same reasons as they are today. Countries and states sought greater lands and valuable resources belonging to other nations. There was a constant struggle amongst nations to emerge as the world's supreme power.

Key Battles

★ **1479 BC Megiddo** Thutmose III of Egypt defeated the kings of Syria and Mesopotamia, marking the highest point of the Egyptian conquest.

★ **480 BC Thermopylae** The hero Leonidas and a small body of Spartans, attempted to stop Persian hordes in their march on Athens. Athens was destroyed.

★ **479 BC Plataea** The Greeks defeated the Persians and ended their attempt to invade Greece.

★ **450 BC Marathon** The Greek commander, Miltiades, with a small force of Athenians and Plataeans, routed a large Persian army, saving Greece from an Asian conquest.

★ **413 BC Syracuse** Syracusans, with help from Sparta, destroyed the Athenian fleet, leading to Athens' defeat in the Peloponnesian War.

★ **405 BC Aegospotami** The Spartan forces captured the Athenian fleet causing the downfall of the Athenian Empire.

★ **378 BC Adrianople** The Visigoths defeated the Romans and settled in the Eastern Roman Empire. This battle broke Roman superiority.

★ **338 BC Chaeronea** After winning this battle, Philip of Macedon gained mastery of all Greece.

★ **331 BC Arbela** Alexander the Great finally defeated Darius III of Persia. Alexander thus became the master of Asia.

★ **216 BC Cannae** A terrible battle in which Hannibal defeated the great Roman army. Rome's existence was severely threatened.

★ **207 BC Metaurus** The Romans, led by Nero, saved Italy from an invasion by the Carthaginian leader Hasdrubal and his army.

★ **49 BC Pharsalus** The decisive victory of Julius Caesar over Pompey. This battle established Caesar as the sole ruler of Rome.

★ **31 BC Actium** A sea battle between the forces of Octavian and those of Mark Antony. Octavian's victory made him the first emperor of Rome.

★ **AD 9 Teutoburger Wald** Germans under Arminius (Hermann) crushed the Roman army commanded by Quintilius Varus. This battle established the Rhine and the Danube rivers as the northern Roman frontier.

★ **AD 312 Milvian Bridge** Constantine the Great defeated Maxentius in this battle. He became the sole ruler of the Western Roman Empire.

★ **AD 451 Châlons** Romans and Visigoths joined together to stop Attila the Hun's advance in France. This battle prevented the Huns from taking over western Europe.

Hannibal and the Battle of Cannae

Hannibal (247–183 BC) was the son of a great general, Hamilcar Barca, who came from Carthage in North Africa. Hamilcar and his army were fighting the Romans in Spain, and Hannibal, although only a young boy, accompanied his father on this journey and pledged that, as soon as he was old enough, he would 'use fire and steel to arrest the destiny of Rome'.

After his father's death, Hannibal took command of the army in Spain. In 218 BC the Roman Senate (or government) made plans to invade Carthage, and Hannibal started one of history's most daring marches. He led his forces along eastern Spain, over the Pyrenees Mountains, and across the Rhône River. His 90,000 infantry, 12,000 cavalry, and nearly 40 elephants travelled all autumn and by the time they reached northern Italy, only about half the army were left.

This did not deter Hannibal, however, and his skilled cavalry tactics crushed the Roman forces at the Trebia River and at Lake Trasimene. Alarmed, the Romans put the wise statesman Quintus Fabius Maximus in charge. Choosing not to risk a battle at once, Fabius instead followed the Carthaginians, delaying and harassing them. At last, in 216 BC, the Roman army met Hannibal's forces at Cannae in South-eastern Italy. Hannibal's army won, slaying an estimated 60,000 Romans.

Hannibal's triumph was brief, however. Neither his own countrymen nor the Italians supported him. His brother Hasdrubal, bringing reinforcements from Spain, was defeated by the Romans and killed. Hannibal finally returned home when the Roman army invaded Carthage. There, at Zama, he suffered a crushing and final defeat.

Great Battles: AD 500 to 1500

★ **732 Tours** Charles Martel and the Franks defeated the Muslim forces known as the 'Saracens'. This saved western Europe from an Islamic invasion.

★ **1066 Hastings** William, Duke of Normandy, defeated the English and became their new ruler. The English king, Harold, was killed in the battle.

★ **1214 Bouvines** The French, under Philip Augustus, defeated the allied English, German, Flemish and Lotharingian forces.

★ **1314 Bannockburn** Robert Bruce of Scotland defeated the English, securing his throne and Scotland's independence.

★ **1340 Sluys** English and Flemish fleets, under Edward III of England, defeated the French and won command of the English Channel.

★ **1346 Crécy** Edward III and English longbowmen won victory over the French cavalry. This battle greatly strengthened England's position in France.

★ **1346 Sempach** The Swiss defeated the Austrians under Duke Leopold. This battle broke Austrian power over Switzerland.

★ **1356 Poitiers** The famous victory of Edward, the Black Prince, over King John of France. This battle ended the first period of the Hundred Years' War.

★ **1415 Agincourt** Henry V of England decisively defeated the French.

★ **1429 Orléans** A young French woman, Joan of Arc, led an army against the English. This battle was a turning point in the Hundred Years' War.

★ **1485 Bosworth Field** The final battle of England's Wars of the Roses. Henry, Earl of Richmond, defeated Richard III. Henry became Henry VII and established the Tudor line of English monarchs.

The Battle of Hastings

The Norman Conquest began with the Battle of Hastings on 14 October 1066. Afterwards, the victorious Norman leader, William, Duke of Normandy (*c.* 1027–1087), became known as William the Conqueror.

William set sail from Normandy with a great army, landing at Pevensey in Sussex, and moving eastward along the coast to Hastings. England's king, Harold, hurried from the north of England with his army of about 7,000 men, many of whom were half-armed, untrained peasants.

The English were tired after their long march, while the Normans were rested and ready to attack. The two armies fought bitterly for a full day. At the end of the day William tricked the English by pretending he had been defeated. When the English dropped their guard, William's army attacked them. Harold was killed and the English fled. On Christmas Day, William was crowned king of England.

The Battle of Bannockburn

Robert Bruce (1274–1329) was crowned king of Scotland after the previous ruler, Sir William Wallace, was executed by the English. After living as a fugitive for many years, Bruce began fighting the English, who had many strongholds in Scotland.

On 24 June 1314, the English and Scottish forces met in the great battle of Bannockburn. England's King Edward II had a much bigger army than Bruce, but the Scottish leader chose a strong position, between the rocky slopes of the Bannock stream and Stirling Castle. When the English advanced they stumbled into pits that had been dug to entrap them and found themselves helpless before the spears of Bruce's men. The English suffered a bloody defeat. Bruce's throne and Scotland's independence were secure.

The Battle of Agincourt

One of the greatest English victories in the Hundred Years' War was won on 25 October 1415, near the village of Agincourt in northern France. The young Henry V had succeeded an insecure throne, and in order to strengthen this, he decided to revive England's claim to the French throne.

Henry's forces landed in Normandy and captured the port of Harfleur. On their way to the port of Calais, their way was blocked by a great French army. The English were greatly outnumbered by the French, but their courage eventually won the day. Each time the French advanced they were forced back by clouds of arrows released by skilled English archers. More than 5,000 Frenchmen were killed, including many princes and nobles. The English lost only 113 men. This decisive battle, along with Crécy and Poitiers, proved the superiority of the longbow over the crossbow.

The Battle of Orléans

During the Hundred Years War, between France and much of Europe, the English occupied most of northern France. The French king, Charles VII, had not yet been crowned because Reims, where the coronation ceremonies for French kings had been held for 1,000 years, was in enemy hands.

A young French girl, Joan of Arc (1412–31), claimed that St Catherine and St Margaret had appeared to her and told her to go to the king, known as the 'Dauphin', and inspire his armies to clear the way to Reims for the coronation. Joan of Arc was equipped with armour, attendants and horses.

When the army moved toward Orléans, her presence filled the soldiers with confidence. From the city Joan of Arc led a series of courageous sallies that discouraged the English and forced them to withdraw. The French victory was celebrated by the first festival of Orléans and the Dauphin was crowned king as Joan stood by with her banner.

Great Battles: 1500 to 1914

★ **1526 Mohács** Solyman the Magnificent of Turkey defeated Hungary, and led his army to the gates of Vienna.

★ **1571 Lepanto** Venetian and Spanish fleets commanded by Don Juan of Austria decisively defeated Turkey in the Gulf of Corinth, ending Turkish sea power.

★ **1588 Spanish Armada** English ships defeated the great Spanish war fleet (the Armada) in the English Channel. This battle ended Spain's mastery of the seas.

★ **1644 Marston Moor** Oliver Cromwell's Ironsides defeated the Royalists and gained the north of England for Parliament. This was part of the English Civil War.

★ **1690 Boyne** William of Orange defeated Stuart forces led by James II of Scotland.

★ **1701 Manzikert Seljuk** The Turks defeated Romanus Diogenes, emperor of the Eastern Roman Empire. The Turks then went on to conquer most of Asia Minor.

★ **1704 Blenheim** English and Austrian troops defeated a French and Bavarian army in the War of Spanish Succession.

★ **1746 Culloden Moor** England's Duke of Cumberland defeated Scotland's Charles Edward (the 'Young Pretender'). This battle marked the last attempt of the Scottish Stuarts to regain the English throne.

★ **1759 Quebec** The British stormed and took Quebec in Canada, securing British domination of North America.

★ **1777 Saratoga** Burgoyne and his British army surrendered to the American general, Gates. The turning point of the American Revolution.

1781 Yorktown The Americans and French commanded by Washington forced the surrender of England's Lord Cornwallis.

★ **1798 Nile** England's Lord Nelson destroyed the French fleet, cutting off Napoleon from France.

★ **1805 Austerlitz ('Battle of Three Emperors')** Napoleon Bonaparte defeated the united forces of Russia and Austria.

★ **1805 Trafalgar** Nelson destroyed the French and Spanish fleets, securing England's sea power.

★ **1812 Salamanca** The English under Wellington completely defeated the French. This battle ended Napoleon's Peninsular Campaign.

★ **1813 Leipzig ('Battle of the Nations')** The defeat inflicted upon Napoleon by allied forces. This battle marked the end of French rule in Germany.

★ **1815 Waterloo** English, Prussians and allies under Wellington and Blücher finally overthrew Napoleon.

★ **1859 Solferino** France and Sardinia-Piedmont, led by Napoleon III, defeated the Austrians. The horror of this battle influenced Napoleon to make peace.

★ **1863 Gettysburg** A decisive battle of the American Civil War: union troops under Meade defeated Lee, forcing his retreat from Northern soil.

★ **1866 Sadowa** The defeat of Austria by the Prussian commander Moltke. As a result, Austria were excluded from the German Confederation.

★ **1870 Sedan** The Prussians forced the surrender of Napoleon III, causing the fall of French Empire.

★ **1877 Plevna** The Russians forced the Turks to surrender this pivotal strategic point, virtually ending the Russo-Turkish War.

★ **1898 Santiago** An American fleet destroyed Spain's Atlantic fleet under Cervera, forcing the surrender of the Spanish army.

★ **1905 Sea of Japan** Japan destroyed the Russian navy and became a world power.

The Battle of Waterloo

On 18 June 1815, Napoleon Bonaparte suffered a crushing defeat near the Belgian village of Waterloo. Napoleon's defeat ended 23 years of warfare between France and other European powers. The battle between Napoleon's forces, which included 72,000 troops, and a combined Allied army of 113,000 British, Dutch, Belgian and Prussian troops was fought so hard that either side might have won.

The British, under Wellington, were retreating to the village of Waterloo. Napoleon overtook them late on 17 June, but because of the heavy rain, he could not attack until the next morning. The battle raged for ten hours. Napoleon repeatedly threw his cavalry against the British infantry. During one furious cavalry charge the French overran all the British artillery.

Wellington awaited help from the Prussians. The French made a last desperate attack but were slowly overcome and admitted defeat that evening. On 22 June 1815, four days after the battle of Waterloo, Napoleon signed an abdication document in Paris. This ended his rule in France forever.

The Battle of Balaklava

The Battle of Balaklava, one of the most famous battles of the Crimean War, was fought on 25 October 1854. It was brought about by an unsuccessful Russian attempt to end the siege of Sevastopol by British, French and Turkish forces. The three armies had laid siege to this Russian fortress to bring the Crimean War to a decisive end.

Although this battle was a victory for the allies, it is famous mainly for the heroic British cavalry charge against Russian field artillery, in which more than one-third of the 673 British troops, commanded by the Earl of Cardigan, were killed or wounded. This was later commemorated in a poem by the English poet Alfred, Lord Tennyson, *The Charge of the Light Brigade.*

The Battle of Bunker Hill

The first major battle of the American Revolution was fought at Bunker Hill in Massachusetts on 17 June 1775. The British had increased their force in Boston and put General Howe in command. Thousands of American troops gathered and the American headquarters sent Colonel Prescott to occupy Bunker Hill.

Prescott, however, occupied the nearby Breed's Hill. On the morning of 17 June, the British were amazed to see trenches crowning Breed's Hill, and began bombarding the fortification. Later in the day the British troops attacked it, but the front ranks were mowed down by American weapons. The others beat a hasty retreat. A third charge by the British was more successful, and the Americans were slowly forced to retreat to Bunker Hill, leaving the battlefield in the hands of the British.

The Battle of Gettysburg

One of the two major battles of the American Civil War was fought at the town of Gettysburg, Pennsylvania, from 1 to 3 July 1863. General Lee invaded Pennsylvania with an army of about 75,000; he encountered the Union Army

of the Potomac (about 90,000 men), under General Meade, on the outskirts of Gettysburg on 1 July. The battle raged fiercely until General Pickett led one of the most famous charges in American military history against the Union centre. Only 5,000 of his original force of 15,000 survived.

Lee watched the survivors return and confessed, 'It is all my fault'. Gettysburg was a disaster for the South and the battle had considerable psychological effect on both the North and South of America, calling forth President Lincoln's Gettysburg Address.

The First World War: 1914 to 1918

The assassination of the Austrian archduke Franz Ferdinand in Sarajevo, Serbia, in June 1914 was the spark that began the 'Great War'. There were already bad relations between Austria and Serbia, and now a war broke out between the countries that would eventually draw in every major power in the world. At the heart of the conflict were two rival alliances: the Central Powers (principally Germany and Austria-Hungary) and the Triple Entente, or Allied Powers (Britain, France and Russia; Italy joined in 1915, the United States in 1917).

The First World War was the first war to be fought on land, at sea and in the air; it saw more advances in technology than any war in history. Machine guns, battleships, land mines, barbed wire, engine-driven transport vehicles, and other products combined with newer innovations such as the aeroplane and poison gas. All these made killing more efficient and the numbers of dead reached terrible proportions.

Key Battles

★ **1914 First Battle of the Marne** French and British forces checked a German invasion, driving them back to Aisne River.

★ **1914 First Battle of Ypres** The British prevented the Germans from reaching Calais and occupying channel ports.

★ **1915 Second Battle of Ypres** The Germans disrupted a planned allied offensive.

★ **1915 Gallipoli** An Allied attempt to knock Ottoman Turkey out of the war and re-open a supply route to Russia. Hundreds of New Zealand and Australian troops were killed.

★ **1916 Jutland** Important naval conflict which took place in the North Sea, when the British fleet forced the retreat of German vessels.

★ **1916 First Battle of the Somme** The English and French led the fighting for five months. They reclaimed a very small area of land at enormous human cost.

★ **1916 Verdun** The French General Pétain successfully defended his fort against the Germans, preventing them from reaching Paris.

★ **1917 Passchendaele** Another Allied offensive at Ypres, in which the ridge and village of Passchendaele were reclaimed from the Germans.

★ **1918 Second Battle of the Marne** A counter-offensive launched by French and American troops. This battle placed the Germans on the defensive.

★ **1918 Second Battle of the Somme** The Germans attacked the Allies, attaining their first major breakthrough since the early days of the war.

★ **1918 Meuse-Argonne** In a battle lasting 47 days, the Americans fought through the Argonne Forest, broke through German lines and crossed the Meuse River.

The Somme

The Battles of the Somme were two encounters fought along the Somme River in northern France. In the First Battle of the Somme (24 June to 13 November 1916), the Allies began an attack on the German line. The British, under Field Marshal Sir Douglas Haig, played the leading role, with a smaller French force. On the first day of battle, the British suffered 60,000 casualties – the greatest one-day loss in the history of the British army. The battle continued throughout the summer, ending in deadlock. Both sides lost in the region of 600,000 men.

The Second Battle of the Somme (21 March to 5 April 1918) was opened by the German general Erich Ludendorff. His purpose was to breach the Allied line before US reinforcements could arrive. German troops succeeded in forcing the Allies back as much as 64 kilometres (40 miles). The Allies assigned General Foch the task of co-ordinating the Allied efforts. He immediately sent French reserves to the Somme, and the Germans lost momentum.

The Marne

The Battles of the Marne took their name from the Marne River, in France. The First Battle of the Marne (5 to 10 September 1914) was a great Allied victory. After major victories in the Battles of the Frontiers (14 to 15 August), the German armies thrust deep into north-eastern France, and were met by newly formed armies in Paris and the surrounding area, under General Joseph Joffre. After a great struggle, the Germans were forced to retreat.

The Second Battle of the Marne (15 to 17 July 1918) stopped the last of General Erich Ludendorff's great German offensives. Although the Germans were quickly stopped along most of the Champagne-Marne front, the Seventh Army broke through Allied lines west of Reims and managed to cross the Marne River. The Allies were soon aided by the arrival of the Americans and within three days the Germans were halted. On 18 July the Allies began a counteroffensive that did not stop until the Armistice on 11 November.

The World at War: From 1918

The end of the 'Great War', did not bring peace to nations around the world. Only 21 years later, the Second World War had begun, and nuclear weapons became the latest development in warfare.

Key Battles

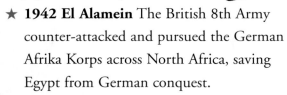

★ **1940 Battle of Britain** German bombers assaulted Great Britain for 58 days.

★ **1942 Coral Sea** In May, planes from US aircraft carriers attacked and destroyed many Japanese warships.

★ **1942 El Alamein** The British 8th Army counter-attacked and pursued the German Afrika Korps across North Africa, saving Egypt from German conquest.

★ **1942-1943 Guadalcanal** US Marines wrested Guadalcanal Island, in the Solomon Islands, from the Japanese.

★ **1942-1943 Stalingrad** The Germans advanced into the Soviet Union. But at Stalingrad (now Volgograd), the Soviets stopped the German drive, then counter-attacked.

★ **1943 Salerno** British troops invaded Italy from the south while American troops landed at Salerno. The two Allied forces joined to liberate southern Italy and to capture Naples.

★ **1943 Tunisia** American, British, and Free French forces pushed through Tunisia and forced the German and Italian soldiers to surrender. This victory freed North Africa.

★ **1944 Bulge** The Germans, commanded by General von Rundstedt, counter-attacked and managed to break through Allied lines in France and Luxembourg. American troops then forced the 'bulge' back and drove on into Germany.

★ **1944 Normandy** On 6 June, Allied troops under American General Eisenhower crossed the English Channel and stormed the beaches of Normandy in France. The Allies then advanced through France into Germany.

★ **1945 Iwo Jima** US Marines invaded the Japanese island of Iwo Jima. After a 26-day fight, the Americans won.

★ **1954 Dienbienphu** A group of Vietnamese Communists surrounded and defeated the French occupiers of a mountain outpost, thus ending the First Indochina War. This led onto the Vietnam War (1955–75).

★ **1982 Falkland Islands** Great Britain and Argentina went to war over this small group of islands. The islands, owned by Britain, are geographically closer to Argentina. Great Britain's Royal Navy eventually defeated the Argentinians.

★ **1991 Desert Storm** When Iraq invaded their small neighbour, Kuwait, coalition United Nations forces performed a defensive to free Kuwait.

The Second World War

The Second World War began in eastern Europe in 1939, when Germany attacked Poland. In 1945, the allied forces of Britain, France and eventually Canada and the USA defeated the German and Japanese forces. Approximately 45 million people, civilians and combatants, were killed.

Battle of Stalingrad

Stalingrad (now Volgograd) in Russia, was the site of a critical Soviet victory. The first phase of the battle lasted from 17 July to 18 November 1942, when the German Army closed in on the heart of the city. Soviet forces under General Zhukov attacked north and south of the city, encircling the Germans, who finally surrendered on 2 February 1943.

Battle of the Bulge

The Battle of the Bulge, or Battle of the Ardennes, fought from 16 December 1944 to 31 January 1945, was Germany's last major attempt to turn back the Allied invasion. German forces under generals von Rundstedt and von Manteuffel drove a wedge (the 'Bulge') into Allied lines through Ardennes. They were halted chiefly by the American armies and forced to retreat.

The Normandy Invasion

The Allied invasion of Normandy began on 6 June 1944 ('D-Day'). The operation, which landed about 1 million troops by 1 July, was under the command of General Dwight D. Eisenhower. The Germans, unaware of the exact invasion point, had 50 infantry and 10 'panzer' (tank) divisions in France and the Low Countries under the command of Field Marshal von Rundstedt.

In the early daylight at low tide about 5,000 Allied ships approached the Normandy coastline. The British and Canadians moved in smoothly at the eastern landing points, and the Americans moved into the westernmost landing site. Within five days, 16 Allied divisions had landed in Normandy, and the final drive to liberate Europe was underway.

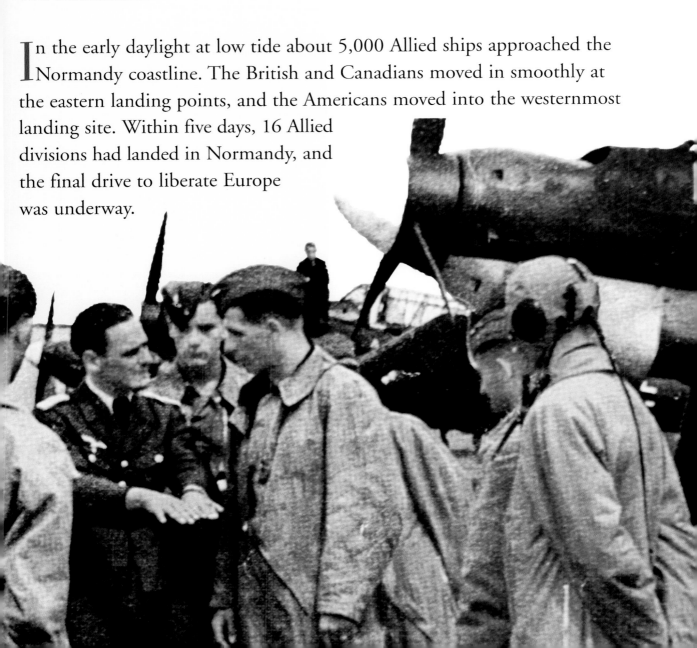

Dienbienphu

Late in 1953, the French occupied a small mountain outpost named Dienbienphu, in North Vietnam. They hoped to cut supply lines and to set up a base from which to attack. The Vietnamese quickly cut off all roads to Dienbienphu, so the French could only be supplied from the air. The French were also taken by surprise when General Vo Nguyen Giap of North Vietnam surrounded their base with 40,000 troops and used heavy artillery to batter the French lines. Despite American aid, the outpost was overrun on 7 May 1954.

By this time support in France for the war had virtually evaporated, and America refused any more aid. The French government sought an end to the fighting, and a peace agreement was signed in Geneva on 21 July 1954. This battle ended the First Indochina War (begun in 1946) and ended French hopes of control in Indochina.

Desert Storm

When Iraq invaded and occupied Kuwait on 2 August 1990, the United States mobilized and led a defensive coalition of United Nations (UN) forces in a campaign called Operation Desert Shield. This was to protect Saudi Arabia and other Arab states from possible invasion by Iraq. The coalition forces were from Great Britain, France, Canada, Australia, Egypt, Saudi Arabia, Syria, and other nations. Iraq's president, Saddam Hussein, was finally given a deadline of 15 January 1991, by which to leave Kuwait. Because he showed no sign of leaving, Operation Desert Shield turned into the military offensive Operation Desert Storm.

For the first 37 days Desert Storm was almost entirely a war of air bombardment. Iraq's military bases and factories were bombed relentlessly from the air and by sea-launched missiles. The ground offensive, Desert Sabre, was launched shortly afterwards, bringing an end to the hostilities.

Great Naval Battles

The Spanish Armada

This battle between Spain (ruled by Philip II) and England (ruled by Queen Elizabeth I) began on 21 July 1588. The Spanish Armada engaged English ships in combat in English waters. The battle was decided by the superior speed and manoeuvrability of the long, low English ships as well as by their long-range firepower. After several major battles, the Spanish boats were severely damaged and, on 28 July, eight of their wooden ships burst into flames. The Spaniards panicked and, when the English attacked again, the Armada fled.

The Battle of Trafalgar

The Battle of Trafalgar was fought on 21 October 1805, off the coast of Cádiz, in Spain. The two sides involved were a British fleet, commanded by Admiral Horatio Nelson, and a French fleet, commanded by de Villeneuve. The British won this battle and, in doing so, established their naval supremacy for the next 100 years.

Battle of Tsushima

This was the principal naval battle of the Russo-Japanese War. The Battle of Tsushima was fought on 27-28 May 1905, in Tsushima Strait, south of the Sea of Japan. The Japanese completely destroyed the Russian fleet. On losing this battle, Russia became the first modern European power to surrender to an Asian force.

Guadalcanal

The Guadalcanal campaign took place during the Second World War, between 7 August 1942 and 7 February 1943. It was a series of naval and land battles at the southern end of the Solomon Islands, in the south-western Pacific Ocean. In order to prevent the Japanese cutting the lines of communication between the United States and Australia, the US marines stormed ashore on 7 August, following a naval bombardment of the island. It took the Americans six months of vicious jungle warfare and seven naval battles to gain control of the seas and subjugate the island.

Great Air Battles

Battle of Britain

In May 1940, many British civilians volunteered to join Home Guard units – a type of land-based army who protected their local community. They were to be the last line of defence against Hitler's forces. A German invasion was expected in September 1940. Hitler's plan (code-named

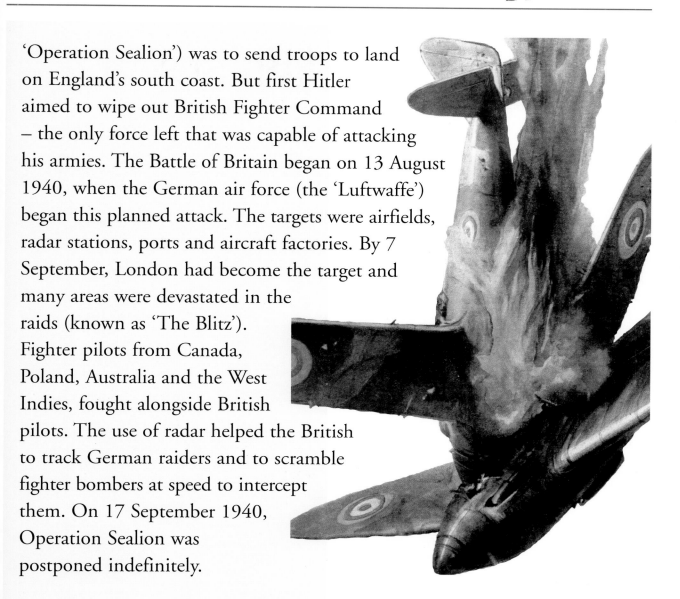

'Operation Sealion') was to send troops to land on England's south coast. But first Hitler aimed to wipe out British Fighter Command – the only force left that was capable of attacking his armies. The Battle of Britain began on 13 August 1940, when the German air force (the 'Luftwaffe') began this planned attack. The targets were airfields, radar stations, ports and aircraft factories. By 7 September, London had become the target and many areas were devastated in the raids (known as 'The Blitz'). Fighter pilots from Canada, Poland, Australia and the West Indies, fought alongside British pilots. The use of radar helped the British to track German raiders and to scramble fighter bombers at speed to intercept them. On 17 September 1940, Operation Sealion was postponed indefinitely.

Battle of Midway

The Battle of Midway was fought entirely by aircraft. It took place on 3-6 June 1942, near the Midway Islands north-west of Honolulu. The American forces destroyed Japan's first-line carrier strength and most of its best pilots. Coming less than seven months after the Japanese attack on Pearl Harbour, the battle turned the tide against Japan and pointed the way to an American victory in the Pacific three years later.

Further Information

Places to Visit

British Museum - Great Russell Street, London, WC1B 3DG. Telephone: 0171 636 1555.

City of Liverpool Museum - National Museums & Galleries on Merseyside, William Brown Street, L3 8EN. Telephone: 0151 207 0001.

Chiltern Open Air Museum - Newland Park, Gorelands Lane, Chalfont St Giles, Buckinghamshire, HP8 4AD. Telephone: 01494 871117.

Hastings Castle - Castle Hill, Hastings, East Sussex. Telephone: 01424 781112.

HMS Belfast - Morgans Lane, Tooley Street, London, SE1 TJH.

Imperial War Museum - Lambeth Road, London, SE1 6HZ. Telephone: 0171 416 5000.

National Army Museum - Royal Hospital Road, Chelsea, London, SW3 4HT. Telephone: 0171 730 0717.

National Maritime Museum - Park Row, Greenwich, London, SE10 9NF. Telephone: 0181 858 4422.

Royal Museum of Scotland - Chambers Street, Edinburgh, EH1 1JF. Telephone: 0131 225 7534.

Science Museum - Exhibition Road, South Kensington, London, SW7 2DD. Telephone: 0171 938 8000.

Tilbury Fort - Tilbury, Essex, RM18 7NR. Telephone: 01375 858489.

Further Reading

All About the First World War, by Pam Robson, MacDonald Young Books, 1996

All About the Spanish Armada, 1588, MacDonald Young Books, 1996

Battle, by Richard Holmes, Dorling Kindersley, 1995

Daily Telegraph Record of the Second World War, Sidgwick & Jackson, 1989

Videos and CD Roms

DK History Encyclopaedia - Dorling Kindersley (CD Rom)
Great Battles of History - BBC (video)
Encyclopedia Britannica - (CD Rom)

Picture Credits

Ann Ronan at Image Select pp. 8, 16
Bridgeman Art Library pp. 14, 15, 17
Christie's Images pp. 24, 26
Image Select pp. 30, 31
Mary Evans Picture Library pp. 27, 29(t), 29(b) 32, 33, 34, 42, 43
Salamander Picture Library pp. 35
Topham Picturepoint pp. 36-37, 38, 39
Visual Arts Library pp. 10, 11, 12, 13, 18, 19, 20, 21, 22, 23, 25, 40, 41
Additional Cover Pictures: *Officier d' Artillerie Galopant à Gauche,* Theodore
Gericault, Courtesy of Christie's Images. *The Battle of Marengo, 14 June 1800,*
Anon, Courtesy of the Visual Arts Library.